Romeo and Juliet: The Coloring Book

Valerie K. Jensen

authorHOUSE

AuthorHouse™
1663 Liberty Drive
Bloomington, IN 47403
www.authorhouse.com
Phone: 1-800-839-8640

First published by AuthorHouse 3/29/2011

ISBN: 978-1-4567-5051-0 (sc)
ISBN: 978-1-4567-5052-7 (e)

Library of Congress Control Number: 2011906427

Printed in the United States of America

Any people depicted in stock imagery provided by Thinkstock are models, and such images are being used for illustrative purposes only. Certain stock imagery © Thinkstock.

This book is printed on acid-free paper.

Romeo and Juliet:

The Coloring Book

Retold by:

Valerie Jensen

Colored by:

You

This coloring book is
dedicated to my friends
of SPHERE.

Val Jensen

November 1, 2010

Once upon a time there were two families who hated each other-

The Montagues

BENVOLIO ROMEO Lord Montague Lady Montague Mercutio

The Capulets

TYBALT   JULIET   LORD CAPULET   LADY CAPULET

ROSaLine   NuRSe

They got into an ugly sword fight in the middle of town.

BENVOLIO
MONTAGUE

TYBALT
CAPULET

Again, and again, and again.

The Prince stops the fight and vows to execute any Capulet or Montague who disturbs the peace again.

After the fight, everyone
wondered where Romeo was.
Romeo did not like to
fight. He liked love.
He was head over heels in
love with Rosaline.

But Rosaline did not love Romeo in that way. She was in love with GOD. She took a vow of chastity and was going to be a nun.

SISTER ROSALINE.

Rosaline broke Romeo's heart. Romeo cried to his best friend Benvolio.

Back at the Capulet's house, the handsome Paris asks to marry Capulet's daughter Juliet.

Lord Capulet got ready for the big party. It was going to be a costume party with singing, dancing and feasting. What fun! Lord Capulet wrote a long list of Capulet's friends to invite to the party. (NO MONTAGUES!).
He gave the list to his servant so he could find them and invite them to the party.

But, there was a BIG PROBLEM.... the Servant Could not Read!

He walked around town looking for someone who knew how to read.

Romeo was still crying about his broken heart to Benvolio. Benvolio tried to give Romeo some advice, and was interrupted by Capulet's servant.

Romeo read the invitation list to the servant.

Signior Martino and his wife + daughters, County Anselmo and his beauteous sisters; The lady widow of Vitruvio; Signior Placentio and his lovely nieces, Mercutio and his brother Valentine; Uncle Capulet, Tybalt and the lively Helena, Rosaline and Livia...."

ROSALINE! MY LOVELY MOON IN THE NIGHT SKY! ROSALINE IS MY LOVE! I WANT TO GO TO THE PARTY!!!

INVITE

Romeo could not believe his good fortune. The servant said Romeo could come to the party as long as he was not a montague. The servnt thanked Romeo and went to invite everyone to Capulets party.

Romeo was so happy to see Rosaline that he did not care the party was at his enemy Capulet's house. Benvolio was excited to go to the party because he loved beautiful ladies, and was hoping Romeo would meet someone new.

At the Capulets house, Lady Capulet asks the Nurse to call for Juliet. She wanted to have an important talk with her daughter.

The Nurse raised Juliet and loves her very much. The Nurse said Juliet was the prettiest babe she ever nursed, and wished she would live long enough to see Juliet get married one day.

Lady Capulet asked Juliet if she wanted to get married. Juliet says NO. No. No!

Lady Capulet wanted to continue the conversation, but it was PARTYTIME... and everyone needed to put on costumes.

Meanwhile, Romeo, Benvolio, Mercutio and a group of other Montagues walked to Capulets house, where they planned to stay for one dance so Romeo could see his beloved Rosaline. The Capulets were their enemy. They hoped they would not be recognized in their disguises.

MERCUTIO   ROMEO   BENVOLIO

Romeo gets very sad on the way to the party. He worries that Rosaline will not dance with him.

Romeo's friends are getting tired of his whining. They make fun of him and try to cheer him up. They are good friends and want to help him get over Rosaline. Romeo has a bad feeling.

The Capulet house was all decorated for a magnificent feast. Capulet was very proud to have the biggest party in all the land. He welcomes his guests and gives a toast.

The guests were all in costume, and everyone was having a ball.

The Montague boys walked in to the Capulet party. Then it happened. Romeo saw Juliet for the first time and was struck by a bolt of love lightning.

HE Did not know her name, or that she was a Cap.

He fell Madly in love with Juliet right on the Spot.

Romeo and Juliet shared their first kiss.

In an instant Romeo fell madly
in love. He forgot all about Rosaline.
He could not control his happiness.
He forgot he was a Montague in his
enemy's house.

TYBALT Capulet recognized Romeo's voice and became ENRAGED!

GET ME MY SWORD! I HATE MONTAGUES MORE THAN I HATE HELL!

Lord Capulet heard Tybalt making a Scene.

Lord Capulet told Tybalt to calm himself down and not to ruin his big party. Lord Capulet was secretly happy his party was good enough to crash. Tybalt backed down, but vowed to get revenge.

Romeo's friends realize that they've been exposed as Montagues. They run away from the party. They drag Romeo with them.

Romeo breaks away from his friends and runs back to the Capulet's house for another look at the beautiful Juliet. Juliet happens to be outside on her balcony talking to herself about how much she loves Romeo even though he's a Montague.

Romeo stepped out of the shadows and declared his love for Juliet.

Juliet tells Romeo that he should marry her if he really loves her as much as he says. They agree to decide if they should get married in the morning.

Romeo ran straight to Friar Laurence's house to ask him to marry him and Juliet. The Friar was working in his herb garden. The Friar was shocked because Romeo was lovesick over Rosaline yesterday!

I want to marry Juliet!

What happened to ROSALine???

Friar agrees to marry
Romeo and Juliet because
he believes their love can bring
peace to the Montague and
Capulet families, and a beautifu
new flower will grow from
the new seeds.

Romeo's friends looked all over Verona to find Romeo. They got a letter from Tybalt challenging Romeo to a duel.

Tybalt was nicknamed the "Prince of Cats" because he was an excellent fencer.

Mercutio and Benvolio made fun of Tybalt because he was very fancy and spoke with a fake accent.

Benvolio and Mercutio
found Romeo - and he was happy!
The friends thought he had
healed his broken heart. They
did not know he was in love
with Juliet!

Mercutio was also an expert fencer.

Benvolio was a lover, not a fighter.

The Nurse finds Romeo in town and asks to speak with him in private.

Romeo tells the Nurse to send Juliet to Friar Laurence's cell that afternoon so they can marry.

Juliet waited impatiently for the Nurse to return.

Finally, the Nurse told Juliet that Romeo wanted to marry her at Friar Lawrence's house that afternoon.

Juliet was so happy
she was going to get Married!

The wedding was going to
be a <u>BIG</u> <u>SECRET</u>.

The wedding hour finally arrived. Romeo and Juliet were very happy. The Friar was afraid that their passion could lead to their doom.

Romeo and Juliet kissed for the first time as husband and wife. Then Juliet snuck back to her parents house. Romeo was going to go for a walk, then creep thru Juliet's window after dark.

Only the friar and the Nurse knew they were married.

The day got hot. Very hot. the Capulets and Montagues got very cranky and started a nasty swordfight.

Romeo heard the screams in the Courtyard. He ran to help his friends, but it was too late. Tybalt killed Mercutio.

Romeo tried to save Mercutio, but he could not. Mercutio's dying words were "A plague on both your houses". He blamed the Montague and Capulet war for his death.

Romeo was enraged that Tybalt killed his best friend.

They fight.

Romeo kills Tybalt. Tybalt was a Capulet. Romeo is a montague...(secretly married to a Capulet). This means trouble. Benvolio tells Romeo to run away or the Prince will kill him.

Romeo run away.

The Prince raced to the scene. He saw Tybalt and Mercutio dead on the ground. He was Furious.

Benvolio told the Prince what happened.

Lady Capulet enters and sees her cousin Tybalt dead on the ground.

Tybalt, my cousin! O my brothers child! O Prince! O husband! O the blood is spilled of my dear cousin! Prince, you must get justice and spill the blood of Romeo Montague!

Lady Capulet did not know that Romeo had secretly married her daughter Juliet.

Lady Capulet blames Romeo and wants the Prince to execute him.

Lord and Lady Montague tried to defend Romeo to save his life.

Do Not Kill Romeo! He was Mercutio's best friend — he only killed Tybalt to get even for Tybalt killing Merc.... Let Romeo Live !

The Prince decided to punish Romeo by exiling him from Verona forever.

The Nurse told Juliet the terrible news about Romeo and Tybalt.

Nooooo! Tybalt was the best friend I ever had!

My husband Romeo was banished? That's worse than 10,000 dead Tybalts!

Nurse! Go find Romeo and bring him to me!

Juliet

The Nurse went off to find Romeo.

Romeo was hiding at Friar's house. The Friar told Romeo he was banished instead of put to death. Romeo thought this punishment was worse than death and cowardly asked the Friar for some poison so he could kill himself.

The Nurse found Romeo at the Friars house. She told Romeo to go see Juliet. This made Romeo very happy.

The Friar told Romeo to sleep over at Juliet's house, then sneak out to Mantua in the morning. The Friar was going to talk to the Prince and try to get him to forgive Romeo. The Friar would send a message to Romeo when it was safe to return.

Meanwhile at the Capulet mansion Paris spoke to Lady and Lord Capulet about proposing to Juliet.

No one knew Juliet was already married -- to their greatest enemy, Romeo Montague!

Romeo and Juliet spent their
first and last night together. When
the sun came up Romeo and Juliet
said goodbye and Romeo snuck out
the window. Poor Juliet did not
know this was the last
time she would
see Romeo alive.

Farewell my love, I will think about you every day, hour and second.

Adieu! Adieu! Someday we will laugh about this.

Juliet was crying for Romeo when Lady Capulet came to her room. Lady Capulet thought Juliet was crying because her favorite cousin Tybalt was killed. Juliet did not tell her mother her tears were for Romeo.

All the tears in the world will not bring Tybalt back.

Lady Capulet offered to have Romeo poisoned to help Juliet feel better. That made poor Juliet cry even harder.

Lady Capulet told Juliet she was going to Marry the handsome Paris on Thursday.

NOOOO!

NO!! I will not marry him !!

I would rather marry your worst enemy!

Juliet was hysterical. Her parents Lord and Lady Capulet were **furious**. Even the Nurse told Juliet to marry the handsome Paris.

Paris was almost unbearably happy to Marry Juliet.

He went to visit the Friar to tell him how excited he was for the big day.

The Friar realized he had a <u>big</u> problem on his hands.

The Capulets threatened to disown Juliet. Juliet did not want to live anymore if she had to marry Paris. She went to ask Friar Lawrence for advice.

I'd rather jump from a tower, or get eaten by snakes or wild bears or be buried alive rather than marry Paris!

Friar Lawrence had a plan. It was very dangerous, but Juliet was willing to try anything.

Friar told Juliet to go home and tell the Capulets she changed her mind and was excited to marry the handsome Paris. He gave Juliet a bottle of homemade poison. He told her to drink it on Wednesday night. The poison would put Juliet in a deep sleep, and everyone would think she was dead. The Capulets would find Juliet "dead" in her bed and would have a funeral for Juliet instead of a wedding. Friar was going to send a message and an antedote to Romeo in Mantua, and Romeo could come back to Verona and rescue Juliet from the Capulet Tomb, and Romeo and Juliet would live happily ever after. Juliet thought this was a <u>fantastic</u> plan.

FRIAR xxx

What could go wrong?

Great idea!

Juliet went home. The Capulets were decorating their mansion for the big wedding. Juliet told everyone she was very happy and excited to marry the handsome Paris. Everyone was happy.

They did not know Juliet had a dark secret

On Wednesday night, Juliet drank the poison.

On Thursday Morning the Nurse walked into Juliet's room. She opened the curtains and let the sunlight in. She tried to wake up the bride-to-be. Juliet would not wake up. Lady Capulet tried to wake Juliet. She would not wake up. Lord Capulet tried to wake Juliet. She would not wake up.

Everyone thought Juliet was dead.

Lord Capulet ordered the wedding preparations be converted to funeral preparations.

The musicians played music to help the Capulets with their grief.

Friar Lawrence went to help the Capulets with Juliet's Funeral.

Only Friar knows Juliet is playing dead. Friar does not know lots more trouble is on the way.

Balthasar was friends with Romeo. He went to Mantua to tell Romeo the bad news that his Juliet was dead. Balthasar did not know Juliet was faking. Romeo did not get a message from Friar Lawrence explaining the plan. Romeo thought Juliet was really dead.

SIT DOWN Romeo, I've got some bad news. It's going to hurt.

BALTHASAR

NOOOOO! I defy you stars! I am going to Verona!

Romeo did not want to
be alive in a world without
his Juliet.

Romeo stopped and bought some
poison on his way back to
Verona.

Friar Lawrence found out that Romeo thought Juliet was really dead. He rushed to the Capulet's Tomb to try to stop another disaster. He wanted to be inside the tomb when Juliet "woke up".

Friar Lawrence was too late.

Romeo arrived at Capulets tomb. He found Paris crying on the steps. Romeo killed Paris because he tried to stop him from breaking in the tomb.

Romeo broke down the door to the tomb. Romeo saw Juliet. He could not believe how beautiful she was. She did not even look dead (because she really wasn't!) Romeo did not know she was in a deep sleep. He thought his love was dead. He wanted to be dead too.

The poison was very strong.
Romeo died. One minute
later Juliet woke up.

When Juliet realized what
happened she kissed Romeo and
Juliet goodbye and stabbed herself
in the heart.

Juliet died in Romeo's arms.

Poor Romeo and Juliet!

Everyone in Verona was sad. The Montagues and Capulets all cried.

They were extra sad that their fighting caused the deaths of their beloved children Romeo and Juliet.

The Prince begged the Montagues and Capulets for peace one last time. The Cap ts and Montagues held hands.

The families lived in peace and harmony for the rest of their lives.

The End.